D1268014

Lines the Quarry

Lines the Quarry

Robin Clarke

OMNIDAWN PUBLISHING
RICHMOND, CALIFORNIA
2013

Cover photo: *Black Cliff, Alberta* © Garth Lenz 2005
Courtesy of the photographer

Book cover and interior design by Peter Burghardt

Offset printed in the United States
by Edwards Brothers Malloy, Ann Arbor, Michigan
on Glatfelter Natures Natural 55# Recycled 30% PCW
Acid Free Archival Quality FSC Certified Paper
with Rainbow FSC Certified Colored End Papers

Cataloguing-in-Publication Data is available from the Library of Congress

Published by Omnidawn Publishing, Richmond, California
www.omnidawn.com (510) 237-5472 (800) 792-4957
10 9 8 7 6 5 4 3 2 1
ISBN: 978-1-890650-89-6

Acknowledgments

Thank you to the publications where the following poems first appeared: "Blessed With No Memory," *Counterpunch*; "Cesar Chavez" and "Mary Harris 'Mother' Jones," *Critical Quarterly*; "'Miner' for 'Minor,'" and "My Mother is a Fish," *Verse*; "The Mine Collapsed Under," *LABOR*; "Everything Wants to Live" and "Type Any Key to Begin," *Word For/Word*. Thank you to Paul LeBlanc's *Work and Struggle: Voices from the Radical Labor Movement* (Routledge, 2010), which served as a resource and inspiration for poems dedicated to specific labor leaders. Thank you to Rusty Morrison, Ken Keegan, and Omnidawn Publishing for bringing this book into the world with commitment and care. Thank you to Brenda Hillman for reading with great generosity. Finally, I am infinitely grateful for the editorial commentary, endless support, and engaged poetics of Emily Carlson, Sten Carlson, Rebecca Mertz, Chris Miller, Daniel C. Remein, Meg Shevenock, and Joshua Zelesnick: without you this book could not have been written.

This book is dedicated to the members of SOCH (Save Our Community Hospitals), including Evelyn Benzo, Tony Buba, Ed Cloonan, Virginia (Ginny) Eskridge, David Hughes, Jim Kidd, Rev. James McDonald, Jan McMannis, Pat Morgan, Carmella Mullen, Mel Packer, Mike Stout, and Scott Tyson. To members of Pittsburghers for Public Transit, including Helen Gerhardt, Paul LeBlanc, Jonah McAllister-Erickson, Marc Mancini, Jibran Mushtaq, and Molly Nichols. To the devoted members of the Thomas Merton Center. To the Pittsburgh IWW. To the Duquesne Adjunct Faculty Association, bringing hope to Pittsburgh's adjunct underclass. To my kind and generous teachers, including John Champagne, Ben Lerner, Dawn Lundy Martin, Greg Morris, Alan Michael Parker, and Tomaž Šalamun. To all the Pittsburgh poets who keep writing into the mess, including Ed Bortz, Emily Carlson, Sten Carlson, Emily DeFerrari, Carolyn Elliott, Rebecca Mertz, Chris Miller, Daniel C. Remein, Meg Shevenock, and Joshua Zelesnick. To Anu. To Nikki. To Kerrylee Hinkson. To Marlo Torrelli. To Maggie Rehm. To Kristi McKim. To Julie Granum. To Walter, Anna, Christine, Marie, and Grace DeForest; my brother, Daryl Clarke; and our parents, the late Linda DeForest Clarke and Robert William Clarke.

Contents

Judge's Citation

Winner of the Omnidawn 1st/2nd Book Prize

selected by Brenda Hillman

Robin Clarke's inventive and brave first collection of poems is not a book that makes you feel better; it is a book that makes you feel. It does not necessarily bring comfort or spiritual discovery—though it could lead to those things. Using an approach that is both collective and personal, the poet meditates on mining culture, on the prison system, on the health care system, on corporate seizure of resources and on systemic economic failure, on attendant environmental disasters; in so doing, she always keeps attention on the specifics of working people and their struggles. The three sequences here are full of detailed fragments of incidents—never completely spelled out—that allude to illness and injury, details of childhood, family history, showing humans and earth as victims of the mines and of both slow and sudden disasters, yet the result is somehow ultimately redemptive.

I chose this book because I admire its combination of soul, ethical subject matter, the texture of its radical style and its language play. Clarke does not maintain an air of detachment despite her indirect and occasionally austere methods. She injects family material in single lines occasionally and with restraint, like a haunting refrain, never self-indulgently. It's not obvious what happened to this family, yet the frequent collage shifts do not evade engagement, and they tell something new about the world.

Clarke joins a style already in progress in contemporary innovative writing, and she does it particularly well; she's not the kind of writer who will leave subject matter and emotion to the side in order to engage in dry sentence shifts. Thus, the work introduces narrative in small bits and enacts current idioms: there is no "single speaker"; the poetry is assembled from paratactic associations, from sentences with shifting "unreliable" syntax, offered by a poet who has probably read both Stein and Ashbery (and who has probably read poets who have read Stein and Ashbery); yet the lines are decidedly less playful than those of Stein or Ashbery. The result is often discomfort and derangement. The poems are cobbled from fragmentary experience, overheard expressions, from synthesized sources, news data, and the result is poetry with a great deal of socio-political "content" and—as the first title indicates—a searing allegiance to the value of the individual experience.

The first sequence in the book makes reference to work in the mines and to a father's incarceration in the prison system ("My Father or the Prisoner Before Him") in ways that seem to intertwine the two conditions. Regardless of how literally one reads the imprisonment of the father, a connection is being made between the work life in the mines and prison. The second and third sequences allude mostly to the failure of the healthcare system to care for urban and industrial workers, to the destruction of life in formerly industrial small towns, and to a mother's cancer. Clarke's modernist and postmodernist fragments seem a profound response to these conditions, as they employ modernist technique that is by now one hundred years old. The title *Lines the Quarry* has a startling appeal; it is a pre-grammatical phrase in which the something interacts with the nothing, meaning is made via the absence of a word or two—a strategic omission. Is it possible a ghostly word or phrase might precede the title? "[Sorrow] Lines the Quarry" or "[Death] Lines the Quarry"? Or, rather, is there something else missing in the phrase itself: "Lines [are in] the Quarry" or "Lines [make] the Quarry"?

The fragmentary nature of Clarke's language is intensely local, as are the figures in the poem an integral part of local mine culture. The poet is part of a community in Pittsburgh where she teaches and where she has worked as a radical activist in support of industrial workers, transit workers and students. Her poetry reflects these inclusive concerns, inviting the reader to a commitment to justice and to beauty. How to make art of concerns for social and environmental justice—without engaging in polemics—is one of the abiding questions for poets now—along with a quest for poetry of vision.

This collection is deft and accomplished. Clarke's lyric shards hold up a shattered urban mirror in a way that has a strong appeal. One continuous motif has directly to do with exploitation of miners and environmental degradation in the mines. Clarke often uses information without trying to make it musical; this impulse is set up by an initial encyclopedic envoi: a list called "2006 Workers Compensation Injury Data":

917 assemblers & fabricators

150 athletes & sports competitors

1,104 car mechanics

4 writers & authors

160 bakers

471 bartenders

1,209 bus & truck mechanics

177 bus drivers

5,417 carpenters

82 carpet installers

There is an apparent stanza break after these first ten lines, followed by another "stanza" with ten more lines, ten more types of workers—six stanzas of ten lines each. The inclusion of the fourth item on the list seems vaguely comic ("4 writers & authors") as if only in very few cases—compared to all other professions—could writing cause injury. Many contemporary poets are using this sort of data in documentary, journalistic, or reportorial poetry. Is this list a poem? It contributes to the poem. The professions and job descriptions are listed dispassionately; the recitation of numbers of the injured quickly blurs, receding in the almost four-dimensional white space of the page, abandoning the elegant lines, betraying the irregular column with its regular stanza breaks. The facts lose informational hegemony as the mind goes numb and ceases to feel—or prepares to feel differently—and something about the list of facts is beautiful.

The materials in the section of the poem that follows have to do with mining, with work in coal, with corporate exploitation, with family suffering, with life between hours of work. The first sentence is more of a sentence-like object and sets the zigzag style and tone: "Everything wants to live, not/even Robocop. The difference/between human, employee/

hired hand & the ocean—/simply the road gets blocked, so/Carnegie built a library/sixteen hours of work each/shift your life is mined/by one way & another/bake a cake between the days,/workers, dynamite, dripping/things you don't want to forget//headlamp, feed dog tied to post." Some might say this style of writing deconstructs capitalist assumptions of progress and hope; others might say its overlapping forms reanimate the lyric by asking it to accommodate to a sound-based, non-smooth music. Both of these may be true; its representations can also be read in terms of adaptation of living creatures. Clarke's phrases act like the parts of insect legs, each with a different function, disjointed—tarsus, tibia, femur—for greater functionality and flexibility; "not/even Robocop" exactly undoes the power of the first declarative clause. At times, I'm reminded of the methods of a rather different poem, Marianne Moore's "An Octopus." This sort of making and unmaking of a phrase-collage continues throughout the collection.

The family's victimization is not spelled out explicitly, even when intensely intimate details are slipped between other kinds of material. The reader is left curious. Prose and lineated verse bring together the experiences of many years and are layered with historical fact. "The mine collapsed under the weight of its many false documents. Today's challenges include 362 ghosts hefting coal into trucks & trains day & night," she writes in one prose piece. The sequences don't push any conclusion, but the book ends as it begins, with a peek at catastrophe and a belief in survival as the ghost drama is played out. I have a lot of admiration for the way this poet makes a relentless but merciful study of an inevitable life force of humans trying to make a living from the earth's dwindling resources; she demonstrates how a collective power can coexist with individual emotive values in language, that poetry can always address—even if it cannot correct—brutal systems. The poet beautifully synthesizes her materials as she struggles with uncertainty and also with compassionate energy.

Brenda Hillman
Kensington, California—Autumn 2012

2006 Workers' Compensation Injury Data, United States

917 assemblers & fabricators
150 athletes & sports competitors
1,104 car mechanics
4 writers & authors
160 bakers
471 bartenders
1,209 bus & truck mechanics
177 bus drivers
5,417 carpenters
82 carpet installers

945 cashiers
217 chefs
407 cleaners of vehicles
1,591 commercial food preparers
1 communications teacher
398 concrete finishers & cementers
4,679 construction craft laborers
229 construction managers
1,060 line cooks
629 fast food cooks

1,185 restaurant cooks
329 cafeteria cooks
575 dishwashers
473 correctional officers
164 counselors
483 customer service representatives

502 driver/sales workers
638 drywallers & ceiling tilers
1 economist
1,851 electricians

3,182 farmworkers
102 fence erectors
436 firefighters
11 fine artists, including painters
10 financial specialists
865 food prep workers
431 glaziers
322 agricultural graders & sorters
1,108 heating & air conditioning workers
2,656 installation & maintenance

1,580 janitors & cleaners
5,260 freight laborers
1,632 landscapers
20 lawyers
626 machinists
1,111 maids
333 medical assistants
276 merchandise displayers
256 metalworkers
282 millwrights

3,023 nursing aides & orderlies
1,035 office clerks
479 operating engineers
470 packers & packagers
625 painters & construction workers

1,207 home care aides

1,360 plumbers & pipefitters

1 podiatrist

7, 532 production workers

870 registered nurses

3,136 retail sales persons

My Father or the Prisoner Before Him

I'm sorry. We're sorry for the massive disruption it's caused their lives. There's no one who wants this over more than I do. I'd like my life back.

—Tony Hayward, former CEO, BP

Everything wants to live, not
even Robocop. The difference
between human, employee
hired hand & the ocean—
simply the road gets blocked, so
Carnegie built a library
sixteen hours of work each
shift your life is mined
by one way & another
bake a cake between the days,
workers, dynamite, dripping
things you don't want to forget

headlamp, feed dog tied to post.
A history of methane
explodes one thousand feet
in your face is a ceiling
coming down? burns ninety
percent of the woman's
disaster porn at Big Branch
coal mine, twenty-nine Do Not
Resuscitates, Mr. Blank
Blankenship throw down a rope
I've got my head but three years
of citation brings the whole
sputtering to today, the
rules, or all Americans
deserve to? The company

Tina pulled levers for
without meaning to,
everything the Titanic
pushes toward, Freud there are
no accidents, whatever
kept us going pegged our pants
& didn't ask how does it feel
to be the Terminator
open fire to open
like a flower on evening
television? To watch
bandaged heads vanish into
parked here forever, soldier
hold your breath you're not crying
right? Good intentions come &
go run up the street with some
adults in need of a bath
tub to slip in, piece of cake
to fall out of a chair
in *five, four* is how I learn
Americans have rallied
round the image of the oil

coated bird but browsers
undirected keep opening
corners of the human package:
seagull, swallow the regulations
the gauzy wings, eye
where security guards feed
dolphins full of tear gas
how do you feel? Purchase
the words for a season

of fishing equipment under
water, clean-up crews have no
time to correxit. "Let's Go"
Shell says, who poisoned Ogoni
land with more oil than BP
pipelines of dead fish, charred
mangrove whisper the secret
every corporation ends
with decisive moments, then drowning
like the wrong number dialed
your ears fill with water then
the stadium applauds
decades of oil, torture, murder
now the people are hacking
into the pipeline
don't click that window
subcutaneous cellulitis
aka beat hand, beat elbow,
beat knee syndrome you are what
they eat. Falling out teeth
dreams say it, together
who did nothing wrong

She worked for many of the cigarettes. A spiritual advisor warned *watch only funny movies*. Is it possible to invent new bodies through television? Like a spell, to bring the childhoods back. We use the present of being we say someone *is* dead. But above Andy Kaufman the young Jim Carrey sings, a balloon strung from the mourner's imaginations. My mother had such affection for zany male actors—I say the phrase a hundred times: *zany male actors*. What are the odds of anything? Exactly the light filtered through the shade as two protagonists die of lung cancer in the threadbare living room that afternoon.

The mine collapsed under the weight of its many false documents. Today's challenges include 362 ghosts hefting coal into trucks & trains day & night. We are not sorry for the miracle parables. At 10:19 am, yours was the most up-to-date model. Don't think we need to tear the system apart. "Great swelling of the Susquehanna" adds something feminine. Alter it, sure. That was blatant, that was intentional. You could just as easily search the internet for smoke & flames pouring from the shaft. Which was the worst disaster since the last one. And finally, dear families, calling them survivors was our mistake.

The opposite would be a candidate available for rejection. Images should be sharp. In twenty-six years, never "went on vacation." The phrase has been popularized by news crews & Warren Buffet. To put your picture in the paper we require residence & occupation. My mother was a cashier & Phi Beta Kappa; my father was an engineer with Hepatitis C. The toll-free number really does not hook people up. When they threatened to take the kids, my Mom chose Listerine not whiskey.

Box of streamers that turn out after all to be snakes. It is difficult to have sex, even with someone you love. The perpetrator becomes your beloved's & later your face. "Ask her if anything happened." To talk about intimate, sad or embarrassing things, simply make lists: time lime grime crime.

"What's the good of prayer?" From the Latin devolvere, *to roll down, fall.* A devotional for inmates, with first names & phone numbers penned in the flap. Work (455-8187). John. Each page bears numbers in the corners. A stick figure devolves into lines. For example 96, 97 & 33, 34 the current year & day of sentence for my father or the prisoner before him. *Still Human!* one meditation begins. Double underlined in pencil: willing to give up the right to yourself.

Cobb 700™ the new standard in high. The new high choice. Value-added, dead-boned broiler, market to market, to buy a fat pig. Poor man's coffin buy a plum bun. White toilet feed slop jiggety jig. The optimist's grow out & pessimist's hog. Performance, the achievement of the highest eviscerated. Home again, home again. Breast meat with the best live. Standard for the misery. Jiggety jog.

Invisible & here are the saddest limitations: self aware & inexpressive. In short, where is the free clinic? As if, always, you have something to offer but what can people count on. To befriend time is a disease, period. After you're released fill the void be productive good that you have these words in your ear, make sure at least one, hopefully two, is it nice to be important or important to be nice? It's the most important & in most cases the hardest part.

She went out at night thinking
herself a failure, like quanta
some light always on between
cracks in the cave. With rhyme,
repetition, stow stories
of girl children young enough
to marry their fathers, old
enough to shoulder the pretend.
Something small left in a yes
or "I don't know" childhood
overflows with powerful
nightterrors nobody talks of so
highly in all the old tomes.

Like a bulldozer goes on
without you, imagine
just one person had folded
your hands, chosen differently
or stayed among the possible.
My mother was born & died
non-prodigy with Picasso
nose, Warhol lips, for five minutes
there was that famous Pittsburgh
haven't-got-time-for-the-pain
in her shoulder from "ringing
the register." It was cancer,
the changes, when I buy shirts
it is still her hands to me
reaching across the counter.
Offered no whole actions
the protestors need no reason
for what they do.

Kitty Dukakis drank rubbing alcohol. According to my mother, as hard as the real thing. Democracy = together we speak with one voice. What is so cheap it is almost real. A way to pass out, eventually? A typewritten letter in the mail from the dentist: *Linda, this is causing fluorosis.* Listerine might be the most shoplifted item in cities. In Russia, known for drinking cheap perfume. To keep the kids, namely. 21.4% alcohol by volume. About the same as Thunderbird. Brake fluid, using a loaf of bread to filter. Kills the liver, then the rest. Stories of antifreeze, "what it was like when."

Who made me were never in the same house when memory starts. Never looked simultaneously at the wall of brown bark & geometric leaves, thinking: *life here before me*. Lives chosen before born, by pre-souls & fracking companies, dump the chemical, buy the mazda, the vacant lot, the southern fan & mandolin hanging from a nail, throw me in the air in the pool before it's gone. Sell the couch, sell it for parts, sell plasma, sell CDs & books from a brain you can't get back, read to me from French books ruined by flood, *Pierre Lapin* or *Peter Rabbit* scrawled on the frontispiece with a huge misshapen *R*. Lives tumbled through, as Rachel Corrie says, *we are all kids curious about other kids*. The poems become jagged—I'm searching for a reason why/when mother & why/when father arrive.

But I'm a pollinator, a teenager shot with holes & light cafeteria on fire. To forget what you're taught, cinch uniform skirt, tell the one about algebra, the window, & gravity. At this school become useful not some busting out of jeans. Butane might be the shortest distance between me & the version on TV. We had lighters & wordiness to slow the strength of nuns when they come, act like you know the combination, run.

Help never arrives so be
where you know how to find you.
These rock graves for instance
never really settle, ash
floats in the collapsed shaft. Let's
liquidate the past, make
individual me's for
the party, two sets of clothes
the ones you came in with
& the ones for burning.
Your parents suffered from what
couldn't be prevented
can somebody please send for

Blessed with no memory
class today is devoted
to pushing your pens back &
across the wreckage. What would
happen if *one woman told*
the truth about her life one
child, rocket, mountain sequel?
A boy with dirt on his face
names the birds at the feeder
Mary, Joseph, baby
those are bruises. Why do we
look less human with each
passing sentence? Walk back &
forth, back & forth find the place
where your desks were.

The women of Harlan County used a cadillac to stop the train. And began singing. Which side are *you* on? I mean, against the caravan of scabs, strikebreakers & police, pushed an extra-long yellow barricade on wheels made by Larry. Meanwhile, a striking miner shot in the head by replacement. The market rides invisible rails like cadillacs my Dad would drive, extra-long Virginia Slims he'd breathe in & draw out, oddly feminine, the asphalt passing neatly beneath his whiskey-paregoric cocktail. Company housing with no running water. Wives picketing in winter coats & loaded guns. A small community of craftsmen founded by Henry Fleetwood of Penwortham, England. He was well-liked & young, with a 16-year-old wife & a baby. The sentences process like waves, always lapping, always returning. My father worked at places where you wear a tie & cologne, but eventually employers stopped calling. As if by being long you ride a float, or a parachute. The Black Lung cases would be incurable. We've come a long way baby cigarettes. Until all the rotten memories vanish into space. It was the '70s, my father lived in high-priced homes, always drinking, driving, but one day they had to pull his body from a boxcar, too.

2010 Workers' Compensation Injuries, Illnesses, Fatalities

3,063,400 recordable cases
933,200 involving days away from work
370,130 sprains, strains, tears
185,270 injuries to the back
208,470 falls

4,547 total fatal injuries (pending)
837 fatal highway incidents (pending)
598 fatal falls (pending)
423 homicides on the job (pending)

In the Building Coming Down

I think the real basis of this thing is that they want to put this hospital in Monroeville...build a $250 million hospital, & there's already a hospital there. It seems they want to go where the money is. And there's the privilege there. The money is there. But they don't want to serve people in Braddock who have medical cards....It really just boils down to if you're poor & you're underprivileged, you have to fight & scratch for every darn thing you want.

—James Kidd, testimony before
the Allegheny County Council,
Pittsburgh, PA, 2009

God or Greed would be the name of the show, Tony said, & the audience votes: natural disaster or CEO? Like lawn furniture during a hurricane, the mining equipment whipped through the air.

What begins as escape? Evenings, or late afternoons, two grooves in the carpet where mom pushed her chair forward or back, depending. Commercial start commercial stop. A job at Kaufmann's was somewhere to be when Dr. Green, her favorite character from long-running TV serial, also had cancer. Have you written a book about television? Coal mining? Diet Pepsi & cigarettes? One thing we all must do is sell our bodies & go to the bathroom. The thing about the children. Will you be putting this on your...? I *am* her charge.

Dad traveled high evergreen walls made of shoplifting, bounced checks, fake prescriptions, prison. The engineering degree from Carnegie Mellon continues to mean something, but what? When you feel embarrassed, think of Oscar Wilde, or Pittsburgh's own Fred Rogers splashing during adult swim. We snagged lipsticks whenever possible, but where is my path? An adult assumes you can simply run across the green lawn, but the simple truth doesn't.

Silence accretes a chrysalis inside which the pupa of "self" kicks on. Eyes, wings, a tail of sorts. The embryo's mother jumps off a high dive, doesn't know what's growing. They had different goals: she wanted to be the baby, he wanted to be the baby. Still, how to explain: the toddler left in the puddle 'til dark, the overheating car crashed in order to cool it.

In Pittsburgh there was alcohol, bath time, & a baby involved. An adult listened at the door. In West Virginia there was "black damp" over everything. Six hours later, who stared glassy-eyed & uncontrollably? The last survivor of the Monongah mine, sitting on his brother's body at the brunt of the cave-in. Without a plan you are just dissociating. One tried to crawl out her window in sleep. So many ways to fall apart, why tell the story? They will have a ceremony, but questions go on for the rest of their lives.

You've been sinking this long, a cruise isn't possible. Her coworkers put some flowers on the plastic grave. The moment I started thought I'd better stop. Life is learning that others are as good or better at what you do. She quit painting but continued smoking & drinking. Zero promises for twenty-six years. I want mom & dad to hold sparklers in the life raft, not death.

Sit & marvel at the pins, waiting to be knocked down in the center. A type of makeshift monument, waiting to be knocked down in the center. To the little arranged bodies, what's done is done, the wrecking ball launched & without intention. At least, that's how the news crews portrayed.

Mining Disasters in the Month of January, United States

1846 Delaware-Hudson, Roof Fall, Carbondale, PA, 14 killed
1883 Coulterville, Mine Explosion, Coulterville, IL, 10 killed
1884 Crested Butte, Mine Explosion, Crested Butte, CO, 59 killed
1886 Almy No. 4, Mine Explosion, Almy, WY, 13 killed
1886 Newburg, Mine Explosion, Newburg, PA, 39 killed
1891 Mammouth, Mine Explosion, Mt. Pleasant, PA, 109 killed

1892 Mine No. 11, Mine Explosion, Krebs, OK, 100 killed
1893 Como, Mine Explosion, King, CO, 24 killed
1895 Butte Hardware, Explosives, Butte City, MT, 150 killed
1902 Milby & Dow, Mine Fire, Dow, OK, 10 killed
1902 Lost Creek No. 2, Mine Explosion, Oskaloosa, IA, 20 killed
1904 Strattons Independence, Hoisting Accident, Victor, CO, 14 killed

1904 Harwick, Mine Explosion, Cheswick, PA, 179 killed
1906 Poteau No. 6, Explosives, Witteville, OK, 14 killed
1906 Coaldale, Mine Explosion, Coaldale, WV, 22 killed
1906 Detroit, Mine Explosion, Detroit, WV, 18 killed
1907 Stuart, Mine Explosion, Stuart, WV, 84 killed
1907 Lorentz, Explosives, Penco, WV, 12 killed

1907 Primero, Mine Explosion, Primero, CO, 24 killed
1909 Lick Branch, Mine Explosion, Switchback, WV, 67 killed
1909 Zeigler, Explosion & Fire, Zeigler, IL, 26 killed
1910 Primero, Mine Explosion, Primero, CO, 75 killed
1914 Rock Castle, Mine Explosion, Rock Castle, AL, 12 killed
1924, McClintock, Mine Explosion, Johnson City, IL, 33 killed

1924, Lancashire No. 18, Mine Explosion, Shanktown, PA, 36 killed
1926 Mine No. 21, Mine Explosion, Wilburton, OK, 91 killed
1926 Jamison No. 8, Mine Explosion, Farmington, WV, 19 killed
1926 Mossboro, Mine Explosion, Helena, AL, 27 killed
1928 Mine No. 18, Mine Explosion, West Frankfort, IL, 21 killed
1929 Kingston No. 5, Mine Explosion, Kingston, WV, 14 killed

1931 Little Betty, Mine Explosion, Digger, IN, 28 killed
1935 Gilberton, Mine Explosion, Gilberton, PA, 13 killed
1938 Harwick, Mine Explosion, Harwick, PA, 10 killed
1940 Pond Creek No. 1, Mine Explosion, Bartlet, WV, 91 killed
1942 Wadge, Mine Explosion, Mt. Harris, CO, 34 killed
1943 Mine No. 15, Mine Fire, Pursglove, WV, 13 killed

1946 Havaco No. 9, Mine Explosion, Welch, WV, 15 killed
1947 Nottingham, Mine Explosion, Plymouth, PA, 15 killed
1951 Burning Springs, Mine Explosion, Kermit, WV, 11 killed
1959 River Slope, Mine Inundation, Port Griffith, PA, 12 killed
1962 Mine No. 2, Explosion, Herrin, IL, 11 killed
2006 Sago, Mine Explosion, Tallmansville, WV, 12 killed

In truth, what happened was
blown up by pilots. My own
"I" a grim consequence
like an olive tree, the
computer said, what protest
could reverse the chain of
unfortunate events?
Want to hear a joke?
I think it may help your work.
Three patients gaze at a fourth
who quietly sips tea. When
the wolf enters, well that
depends what you mean by a real

velveteen rabbit back to life.
A thinking in the feet
entirely flat, bottoms
out & we don't know the cuts
shells made underwater,
wonder could there be an ocean
floor? The answer not visible
makes you grow up quick, cliché
—Dear CEO—but true
if you need someone to brutalize
or sell, one who listens
& is never some stolen
jewelry or gamble on boxing
we need more time

(Rodriguez, et al.). No razed
hospital in Braddock, Pennsylvania
will erase the early stages.
Our disease, when revealed, the
doctors were at home watching.
Dear universal ailing
lifelong resource, what does rapid
pulse & the individual
"my life" have to do with it?

Thank you for the amazing
questions, they don't count for much.
Dear comrades: the action of
going to houses &
delivering signed/sealed
valentines has been canceled.
This does not mean you should
relax: read the findings here
here's the triple bottom line:
soap operas are terrible
but popular materials
previously considered waste

Strike! is a verb that can crawl
like a baby or roll flaming
canisters down the boulevard.
Conceptual alternatives:
give the people back their
hospital, the steelworkers
built it one paycheck at a time,
start flying doctors instead
of powdered milk for infinite

rolling admissions
straddling two or more states
of emergency is what
being a doctor/demo-
cracy/documentary
is all about
demolition. I didn't
always think this way but
BP Shell Oil Bristol-Myers
Squibb DuPont Merck Eli
Lilly Geneva Chevron Ted
Turner Boeing Smith &
Carnegie Steel Wesson
Walmart Exxon Bill
Cross Blue Gates UPMC
Mellon DOD Contracts
Union Carbide Warren
Buffett Gulf's Marcellus shale
mosh-pit reinvented
the social. In my garden
Marxism we'd all wear silk
ties if we wanted. Dear
Malcolm X, when will we know

Egypt is in Africa?
Market conditions: mortal,
need food, drink, shelter
though many'd hand you a shirt
in a storm, circle where their
town used to be. Abnormally
high rates of asthma, please turn
away from where an ER

used to be. "They will stay
in their trap as wage laborers
or tenants. The have-nots
(well, pottery, a few books, one ornamental lamp...
What do you love about this
world? Without what is there nothing

else to say? Kevin Costner's
rock band, Kevin Costner's oil
centrifuge, Kevin Costner's
ark where the animals
anywhere they want to go?

This study examines personal
health record systems (PHR)
data will be gathered
which has no importance
"a press clipping,"
"a neutral phrase,"
one or more choices
to apply to Loyola
not for its stellar rep but
the be-you-ti-ful city
of Chicago. I embark
on the arduous task of
success, unfortunately
destroying your interpretation—
the child wearing the
General Braddock costume
for instance, when the bulldozer
comes. Position: worker,
like the fish who was first a

being-for-itself, later
an object, finally the
model for a short story
without verve or central themes:
you were hoodwinked & hooked,
you took the bait—the end.
Write thank-you notes for the
speakers in advance
Violin ♩♩♪

Voice
In grammar, relation of
the subject to the action.
He hates to complain. Hard Times
Is/Are Fighting Times. Whose Side
Are You On? The valve closes
to stop the flow. The Carrie
Mill was so close if I rolled
down the backyard & hit a bump
promptness, respect, eating,
sleeping, cell phones must be turned
off. If you are so tired
I'd have landed in the furnace
you can't stay awake, good luck
keeping your job, probably
fingers, best to tackle them assembly
line style, start ahead of
time, have the kids write their names
on a heart & glue. I did
write to Elijah Muhammad
who lived in Chicago
6116 South Michigan Avenue.

Lines the Quarry

Genora Johnson Dollinger

Under the category of weapons, can anyone imagine cuntface, cuntface, a hundred-woman strike brigade walking past a line of Pinkertons, rifles & cops to the auto factory floor? In 1936 or 2012 that's Captain Cuntface to you, you have to wear it, like a body, stitched into the mirror itself: they won't shoot you in the back. As in the history of wardrobe, doing is being, not to mention those hairstyles. Wooden clubs for hands, car-seat leather into wristbands. And we can, under the category of weapons, unsew a stitch for the new world. They grab the jacket's back just slip right through.

To answer your questions, I do not require rights. The book makes parallels between miners & children, marriage & televisions. Sometimes humans love—need—machines—to resemble them. I think the boy woke every morning with a phantom bullet piercing his spine. The image will appear in the middle of the poem. Frick called the assassination attempt *my accident*, but it should have been *my life*. It is a book about oil. I will not profit. A book about my father, though he did not work for the Defense Department, as many fathers do. The woman in the wedding dress is not my mother but does appear in the family record as *Linda*. Our family pictures were kept in a plastic bag. The relationship between words & image is an ancestral fan, accordion style. Not yet accepted by a publisher. Especially if that is expensive.

A. Philip Randolphe

Not only have we met no winners, we have met no persons who have met winners. How to strike with a union I was barred from joining? Things have happened in the army/school/factory contains in itself accumulated anger of the whole. Either robbing your own grave or digging it. The Socialist Party has opposed all forms of invisible man. Still, the union to Negro workers has been an unhappy marriage, empty in the eyes. The line break, call it melancholy. Along with total destruction of the Red Cross, demand the people's community control of love, hate, death, land, bread, housing, peace.

Cobb 700, 49 days old, 5.9 lbs

A change in shape can alter the forces

A problem called "livability"

The new weight places strange demands on the immature skeleton

Percent eviscerated yield, 72.565

Gait scores 3 & above: widespread lameness

Most of the 48 billion broiler chickens come from three parent
companies

"Broiler chickens"=chickens raised as meat

Targeting rural areas where unemployment is high

1916 Robert Cobb Sr. buys the Old Pickard Farm in Littleton, MA

Percent breast actual, 23.411

Feed restriction programs: every day, or skip-a-day, or skip two or three
days

71% of poultry farmers earn below poverty wages

Take a look in your local supermarket—they are one of the popular meat
breeds

1947 Cobb begins a breed of all-white birds called "White Rocks"

Commercial Trial 1, Cobb 700, livability 96.33

Arsenic, ammonia, & other chemicals found in feed

1959 the first Cobb Franchise opens in Europe

New ventures in Argentina, the Philippines, Thailand, Hong Kong,
Brazil, Peru, Venezuela, Ireland

1964 distribution into "Africa" begins

1974 Tyson acquires the breeding lines

1998 Cobb Germany formed

2001 Cobb Europe formed

OSHA cited Tyson after an employee was asphyxiated by off-gassing
decaying organic matter

A federal judge granted class action status to a lawsuit regarding massive
numbers of undocumented workers

During a national day of protest for immigrant rights, Tyson temporarily
closed nine plants, anticipating a lack of workers

2008 Tyson continues its "investments in the Brazilian poultry industry,"
buying three poultry companies in Southern Brazil

With Hendrix Genetics & the USDA, awarded $10 million genomes
grant

Purchase of TimberLake farm in Texas to house great grandparent level
multiplier flocks to provide for increasing worldwide needs

Most are in a state of constant hunger

Who are you after they leave? This is Robocop's dilemma. When his workers wanted to go to the segregated pools, Carnegie built a library & taught the second hand to wait. This epic film will stage the final battle between Henry Clay Frick & the Homestead zombies. Names like "John," "Jane," & "Charlie" for the strikers because beyond historical reference.

On January 3, 5, 6, 11, 17, 19, 20, & 30, no one was killed by a mine explosion. Abilify is not for everyone. Commercials embarrass me. Mom did not have this problem. She was dying, which gave her an argument. 1,699 people killed in the month of January by various mines. What is an accident? Eight in Pennsylvania, eleven in West Virginia, six in Colorado, five in Illinois, four in Oklahoma, two in Alabama, one in Indiana, one in Montana, one in Iowa. To the teller when the checks bounced, *I am who they are written for.*

When all the joints stand in for disease, that's poetry, but I didn't read it. Vibration White Finger, Hand & Arm Vibration Syndrome, years of power tools while working for the famous jet engine manufacturer. Your open palm the only proposal for change—too much problem, or a knock. To assure everyone, studies remember Francine & her father, the occupational deafness, sawdust asthma, benzene-xylene-toluene leukemia, bad bosses are bad for your heart. We're going to see pockets in this country, a reality series where disasters from around the world, then the audience votes.

Chickens do. Chickens do not. The guard did. What? The guard was. Cry. Cut the neck in your back kitchen tragedy.

Troy. Troy Davis. Troy Davis was. Troy Davis was innocent. Chickens do not. Yes they do. The bald eagle wouldn't. Troy Davis was. Troy Davis was innocent. Innocent on. Troy Davis was innocent on Wednesday. On his cot. On Thursday Troy Davis was. Was not.

Never allowed his say. Chickens do not eat other chickens. Yes they do. Edible companions. Cot. Dirty, dumb, overly abundant. Troy didn't kill Officer MacPhail. Put the middle name back in, make him a charismatic weapon. Gallus gallus domesticus. Sodium pent. Doesn't make you feel. Doesn't make you feel less. From the dictionary of received ideas, doesn't make you feel less left out. The opposite of hospitality? It's about community. Sales, a practice of sustained. Attn: Cobb 700. Thrown out.

One woman sleeps in the quarry
One man lies with the ore

They wake, chronologically
in order of departure

want to purchase too much
swedish fish, gummy worms, pot

the start of spring is something
medicinal to take the pain in

between biographies, they
are in the world but not of

it, a film out of camera
feeling for all record of

I think &/or am
under black damp completely

correct to wonder why paint
this Brueghel in the slag heap

Father, daughter, mother, son
what do you see as details

what do you see as derails
This makes you human, this

Dear New York Times, I got married six times. This will be seven. Dad played the mandolin, or "Mandolin Wind." He shot heroin through the '90s, or bought me a puppy. He was married five times or six. We laughed at his photograph with the perm, or he drove the car on the sidewalk.

There were underpants, a secret shack, bottle caps, nails, hands involved. Oprah says you can say only "Yes" or "I don't know." One of them is only five. It is what you think. Why tell the story? Because, who are you after they leave?

I never had a chance how can that be barely legal? The meaning appears in the most unbearable case. You will be executed. Democracy from the Ancient Greeks, war can be waged like a hand of poker. I wish you would speak from more clearly. Even the Greeks had gods this is not the problem. Panic whom we address literally & offer bowls of olive oil, split goats, oxen at the altar had no sense of accumulation for its own sake. In my town what is depressing the teens? Human all too human, something's got to give. You will be executed. A concept of reciprocal exchange known as tit for tat. The Greeks drew their police force from slaves. Democracy Where. We, as a group live. In the unmanned pockets one hopes to say "I" & feel unashamed. The man is not homeless, his home *is* the park. The legality of behavior rides on who's speaking. Who's speaking? You will be executed.

Samuel Altieri

John Baloga

Benjamin Boyer

Francis Burns

Charles Featherman

Joseph Gizenski

Dominick Kaveliskie

Frank Orlowski

Eugene Ostroski

William Sinclair

Daniel Stefanides

Herman Zelonis

In 1984 Los Angeles, the nearest child manipulates a garbage truck with a joystick. On one hand, marvel what the cyborg can do & the human can't. Who starts a car using only its fingertips? Still, only half-human, he stands out as the most human of all.

Against all instinct, Sarah Connor befriends the Terminator & it is called holy matrimony. A crab climbs out of a pool of oil. It cannot be done all immediately. Kevin Costner drops sandbags to the ocean floor. Am I those pigs you've roasted on a spit? Crew member hugs loved one. Skimmers collect dark streaks. The anti-submarine will be used, I suppose, to kill the oil? I'm not a white horse nor am I on a white horse, said Costner. I want my life back. As if an epic event happens every episode—as if to restore the way it was before.

Mom said write one page every
day & like Johnboy you'll have

a bright cloud following, but
she didn't know how to paint

three hundred years into one
Spanish Madonna. How to

convey that life cuts off? Baby
gets its own food before bed

before it ends. The rhythm
of these poems meant to

replicate a seed in shallow
dish will bloom fingernail sized

harvests, so take the high road
expression, the work began with you

number two one three nine two
two, please don't remove

the cornerstone without
texting me first the details—

definitely sad the plants
can't ride recycled bikes

to your funeral, but why
write a "good" not cryptic

speech? Press liquify for the
body, find a seven letter

word interchangeable with
wait, the human party, I'm late

In the final episode
he cannot after all give
them eternal life, only
mardi gras across remains
where babies once edged out
& bodies radiated
with insurance. Those days, mom
took the bus to sell Jones New York
outfits, Robocop was seen—
many old ladies bought
sweaters on social security
returned them weekend next—
it was something to do
this Karen Carpenter tune
went on for a year, cancer
the thirteen story Kaufmann's
giant outdoor numerals
drivers honking more now
now that the couches are
actually burning

piss, things you'd rather forget
more ash
machine grease
chicken bones

a small Jeanne d'Arc
6,147 words
super glue for stitches
hand warmer

Fucccccckkkkk U
one apology
library card
fishing line

a blue balloon piece
silt
state-issued ID card
empty mouthwash bottle

man's underpants
toilet paper sheet
what it's like to soil your own pants
wrong kind of look from father

nighterrors nobody talks of
a little doodle
heel of bread
crow

cigarette butts
sweatpants
band-aid
excavator

diet pepsi
prescription bottle
cassette tape
diaper

Linda DeForest Clarke, 54 years old, ~125 lbs

But not always

She was younger & ate more chips

Age 11, father dies of heart attack in courtroom

Unfiltered tobacco & Bob Dylan

Inherited traits such as eye color

Over 50 carcinogenic substances in tobacco smoke

11 proven to cause cancer in humans

7 probably cause cancer in humans

49 of the substances cause cancer in animals but have not yet been
proven to cause cancer in humans

This makes you human, this

But not always

"If I knew I would feel like this, I never would have started"

Cancer is depression eating the body from the inside

But not always

Some people just get it

This

Alters brain as well as behavior & mood. Used in insecticides.

This tar to tarmac roads

Tell about effects of cashiering

Arsenic. Cadmium & nickel used in batteries

This, this

All day standing in place

Toluene, found in hydrofracturing, paint thinners. Known to produce memory loss

So that the cashier has a choice of whether to stand or sit down

Vinyl chloride used to make vinyl products

Creosote

This formaldehyde to preserve necrotic tissue

As the day goes by it gets scribbled & canceled

My mother thought the pain in her arm was from ringing the register

Polonium 220 causes cancer of the liver, cancer of the bladder, stomach ulcers & leukemia

The treatment shouldn't be worse than

What is the disease?

Retail among the fastest growing industries

The effects of cashiering on tobacco sales

We do not speak of the cashier's ire

Acetone—a nail polish remover

Few customers behave politely or reasonably

Cyanide used to kill rats

Heel spurs

To push & give your best. To rest & know how to recharge your
batteries

A little break technique I call "clean up my to do."

But it was a tumor, pressing on her neck & shoulder

Twice as likely as white collar workers to smoke tobacco

Mining, food service, construction, retail

My knees kill me after a couple eight hour days in a row

Take a break by making a new list & if time permits at the end of the
day, make the list for tomorrow

My mother is a fish
my father is a car

the book is blank
with acts one never could

by the time I was born
Terminator no longer

wanted anything except
work (455-5533)

ancestries, German Irish
Slovak Italian Polish

English (3.6%)
this is your reward for

pumping all that money in
the engine: historical

styles of drinking for the mass
production of then we could

"Minor" for "miner," bulldozer
for "working up alternatives"

how many engineers get
hepatitis C after all?

How many cashiers *cum laude*?
Your case may be isolated

call me president of
evasive answers, it's true

my grandma took the dashes
from Emily Dickinson's

so I could be born
safe slash sound where the kids are

often nine but never cry
when little lovely ends

just pretend, text the corpse, don't
think I'm that smart, praying

waist deep in the speed of light
is the rocket that could launch

a thousand Donald Ducks
Mickey Mouses, waves, whatever

When two spine surgeons marry, that's the 1%. But the child's bedroom opens & what astral body steps into the light? Over millions of years, the Rocky Mountains lifted. Tectonic plates pushed 300 workers up out of the mines. The math of human energy: for every labor leader shot in negotiations, eleven strikers' wives press pistols under winter coats. When history points to the massacres, the "death special," the tent city sprayed with bullets, talk directly into the book: on the last day, eighty-two troops refused to go.

Is it really rape when
type any key to begin
annotating the annotated:
my father was raped in a quarry
age five by friends of the fam'ly,
Carnegie's many faces
fill a steam engine book
of men who climbed out of hist'ry—
my body neither shame nor bliss
simply try, their words come out
cursive in the margins
oil in the ocean where
cities build over the last
ones. Don't know what it means
I was born on a business
trip, suspect everything.

Male, anal, oral, don't
count as rape, look at my cell
what do we see? Illusion,
no distance between our lives,
bonds—terrible, & standing
up for what we be. Flush
sediment toilet, balls
to the wall smart but nobody
knows my name. How to define

penetration? Yes, let's grade
your painting of a lighthouse
scene. You can't stay neutral
on a moving train, the bus
leaves at eight there won't be
another. Mom knocked three times
but the door to the human

party was let's just say nope.
Hope this ends better than the
play. Crack the following,
a roach in every pot,
twenty-four/seven
community oriented
lice. When I return we can
marry, exchange relatives
—we'll see—when I see
Emily Dickinson staring
with the worker's carcass
steady as she gathers
at the liver. You've got to
listen to your part. Many
like her yet no two alike
my journey to the center
of the earth begins with movies
but the cashier's decisions
have been left out. Mom'nDad
could not cross that gravel room.
How a child connects most
fondly with the Terminator
those affected I'll go ons

Cesar Chavez

You take a job for security
but the job is to build your
own coffin, gray wood & nails
skip middle age entirely.
Fight poverty with
security, except
fatigue, shortness of breath
methyl bromide–dusted eyeballs
hanging on the vines
children who live near the vines
parents who work in the rows
the tallish rows whose silhouettes
at dusk suggest a human
cluster whisper secrets
of the jams & jellies
the juices & the raisins
resveratrol inhibiting
cancer in the Kennedy's
(tannins & time a wine spends)
the strike now is spiritual
the poverty a praxis
a tradition called *pigeage*
à pied with both feet stomp
the must of this pig age.

Cigarette, bathroom, affordable meaning what can you live with. Andy Kaufman died from mom's kind of real. Can this be called a situation-comedy? Having worked in the thirteen stories department store, I know it is important to say the women's last names. You have written a book about *M*A*S*H*. Will you be putting this on your charge? Dr. Green came out of the television: *Linda, every time I see an orange popsicle I will think of you.*

Mary Harris "Mother" Jones

What to do when yellow
fever, husband, child, child
child, child? She may have lived
100,000 years, a marriage
of action verbs & explosives—
the more I think the more rad
I get—mops & brooms used to
barricade the mine entrances
nobody wants a lady
to march one hundred child workers
from Philly textile mills to the
President's house on Long Island
so she must become the most
dangerous America itself

The history of human expression (liquid) we are not quite prepared for the blows. Also require information on the couple's parents. The census records 5,220 burglaries, 15 murders, 75 rapes, the worst performing school in the State of Pennsylvania & 7,000 human beings. Many of my fondest memories are indistinguishable from where the final battle was actually shot. Devoted to wealth, local libraries, scientific research. My mother & father stand next to each other with beer cans. The wreckage floats as story, stories that never fit. Please include this information even if the patterns are no longer living. Many inmates have been martyrs, many abused, some recognized, some fell asleep & thought they were lords. Describe the times when you knew. His life has often been referred to as a true story.

Who will say the curses now
in the quarry? Take lupus

a baby or diabetes
what's the difference when

you're diagnosed on the sidewalk
between violence & skill

how long does a heart attack
how much is a poor person

traveling in Pittsburgh for
stitches or another speech

delivered in the street
where Tony gets a new idea

for a film: boy rides shopping
cart down Braddock Ave until

it crashes. As when my mom
burned the first layer, then the

whole mattress, *shitfuckpissdamn*
I think is the missing link.

Robin Clarke is a poet, activist, and teacher in Pittsburgh, Pennsylvania, where she has lived most of her life. She is a non-tenure-track faculty member at the University of Pittsburgh, a member of the Pittsburgh Industrial Workers of the World, Save Our Community Hospitals, and the Thomas Merton Center, and she is a strong supporter of single-payer health care. Her poems have appeared or are forthcoming in *Conduit*, *Counterpunch*, *Critical Quarterly*, *Fence*, *In Posse Review*, *A Joint Called Pauline*, *LABOR*, *Lafovea*, *Sentence*, *OWS Poetry Anthology*, *Whiskey and Fox*, and *word for/word*. With the poet Sten Carlson, she has coauthored a chapbook entitled *Lives of the Czars* (nonpolygon, 2011). She would be nothing without the exceptional community of writers and friends whose solidarity make this life possible. You can read work by her and Pittsburgh writers she admires at burghforoneto.tumblr.com.

Lines the Quarry
by Robin Clarke

Cover and interior text set in Syntax LT Std and Garamond Premier Pro

Cover photo: *Black Cliff, Alberta*, © Garth Lenz *2005*
Courtesy of the photographer

Cover and interior design by Peter Burghardt

Omnidawn Publishing
Richmond, California
2013